1

© Knowledge Books and Software

The First Peoples of Australia
came over a long time.

© Knowledge Books and Software

3

© Knowledge Books and Software

There were people of the deserts.

© Knowledge Books and Software

© Knowledge Books and Software

There were the small people
who lived in the rainforests.

© Knowledge Books and Software

7

© Knowledge Books and Software

Tasmania had people who walked there when the sea was low.

© Knowledge Books and Software

9

© Knowledge Books and Software

There were nations of different people.

© Knowledge Books and Software

11

© Knowledge Books and Software

They spoke different languages.

© Knowledge Books and Software

13

© Knowledge Books and Software

Music, dance, art, speaking, and markings were special.

© Knowledge Books and Software

15

© Knowledge Books and Software

Some areas had lots of food and water.

© Knowledge Books and Software

17

© Knowledge Books and Software

People moved to where food was found.

© Knowledge Books and Software

19

© Knowledge Books and Software

Some places had very little food and water.

© Knowledge Books and Software

21

© Knowledge Books and Software

The first peoples had many
ways to hunt and gather food.

© Knowledge Books and Software

23

© Knowledge Books and Software

Word bank

Tasmania

Australia

people

desert

rainforests

different

languages

music

dance

art

speaking

special

markings

found

gather

© Knowledge Books and Software